# YOUR KNOWLEDGE HAS

**Bibliographic information published by the German National Library:**

The German National Library lists this publication in the National Bibliography; detailed bibliographic data are available on the Internet at http://dnb.dnb.de .

**Imprint:**

Copyright © 2016 GRIN Verlag
Print and binding: Books on Demand GmbH, Norderstedt Germany
ISBN: 9783668695283

**This book at GRIN:**

https://www.grin.com/document/424005

Alireza Naimi

# An innovative approach to solve the network design problem concerning intelligent vulnerabilities

GRIN Verlag

**GRIN - Your knowledge has value**

Since its foundation in 1998, GRIN has specialized in publishing academic texts by students, college teachers and other academics as e-book and printed book. The website www.grin.com is an ideal platform for presenting term papers, final papers, scientific essays, dissertations and specialist books.

**Visit us on the internet:**

http://www.grin.com/

http://www.facebook.com/grincom

http://www.twitter.com/grin_com

**An innovative approach to solve the network design problem concerning intelligent vulnerabilities**

Word Count:
Number of Tables: 1
Number of Figures: 7
Total Count: = 5,750+ (7 x 250) = 7500
Date Submitted:


Submitted for Peer Review and for Compendium of Papers CD-ROM at the Annual Meeting of the Transportation Research Board (TRB) in January 2016, and for Publication in the Journal of TRB

# 1. ABSTRACT

In today's congested transportation networks, disturbances like crashes may cause unexpected and significant delays. All transportation networks are vulnerable to disruptions, to some extent, with temporary or permanent effects. Vulnerability is more important in urban transportation networks, due to heavy use and road segments that are close to each other. Small disturbances on an urban transportation network segment can have a huge impact on its accessibility. Intelligent adversaries may take advantage of these vulnerable parts of the network in order to disrupt the transportation operations, and increase the overall transportation cost for the users.

Often, the decision of improving the networks in transportation planning and management tasks are made without adequately taking into account the possible vulnerabilities. By considering the factor of vulnerability in their decision, planners could prevent severe unforeseen disruptions in the future. Robustness is defined as the extent to which, a network under disturbances is able to maintain its function for which it was initially designed. This study proposes an innovative model for designing robust networks against intelligent attackers. In the model, three decision makers are considered: the network manager/designer, the adversary (intelligent attacker) and the users of the network.

## 2. INTRODUCTION AND LITERATURE REVIEW

Design of robust networks are the attention of many researchers. However, until now there is not a universally accepted definition for the vulnerability of networks (Snelder, n.d.). Robustness is the opposite of vulnerability. Therefore, a network that is vulnerable is not robust and vice versa. The main contribution of this paper is a new methodology for designing robust networks strategically, by considering an intelligent adversary entity, who attempts to exploit the vulnerabilities of the network to the maximum of his or her capabilities. The most appropriate way to model the vulnerabilities as a result of intelligent disruptions, could be to model them as a player in a game that tries to achieve his or her objective(s). Some of the studies focused on operational network design. However, the strategic network design against vulnerabilities needs to be further studied. In addition, despite the works that have been done to design robust networks against stochastic vulnerability, this approach could provide new ways to analyze the vulnerabilities in networks in a higher level of detail.

Since three decision makers are considered in this study, the possible associated models and objectives are reviewed. First, a brief introduction to the game theory is provided followed by a review of the network design problem (NDP). From a design point of view, the designer may have multiple objectives when improving the performance of a network such as total system cost, robustness against reliability and vulnerability, reduction of pollution emission, and multiyear investments. On the other hand, from a user perspective, they look for their optimal route choice, mode, and destination. From an adversary view point, the objective is to degrade the performance of network to the maximum of his capabilities. Hence, a design for a robust network must consider the alleviation of potential disruptions.

Finding the optimal road design has been the subject of transportation studies for a long while, and is known to be one of the most complicated problems in transportation. A large number of formulations and solution algorithms have been presented over the last 50 years to solve complex mathematical programs (Chiou, 2005a; Leblanc, 1973; Murray et al., 1998; Suwansirikul et al., 1987).

Network design problems are usually modeled as multi-level models. Multilevel programming, which has received significant attention during the last few decades, is a branch of mathematical programming that can be viewed as either a generalization of minimization-maximization problems or as a particular class of Stackelberg games with continuous variables. The network design problem with continuous decision variables, representing link capacities, can be cast into such a framework. Marcotte (Marcotte, 1986) gives a formal description of the problem and then develops various suboptimal procedures to solve it. Gradient based methods were used (Chiou, 2005b) to solve a continuous network design problem in a transportation network where Wardrop's first principle was used for traffic assignment. Bi-level optimization problems have shown that they are non-convex and difficult to solve using exact optimization algorithms (Konur, Golias, & Darks, c2013) (Golias et al., 2013; Konur & Golias, 2013).

Further research has been done to find more efficient heuristic algorithms, which may give near optimal solutions or local optimum solutions (Allsop, 1974; Steenbrink, 1974). Methods like equilibrium decomposed optimization EDO (Suwansirikul et al., 1987), which are computationally efficient but result in suboptimal solutions and not suitable for large real networks problems. Gershwin et. al. (Gershwin et al., 1979) formulated the continuous network design problem (CNDP) as a constrained optimization problem in which the constrained set was expressed in terms of the path flows and performed their method on small networks. Marquis (Marcotte and Marquis, 1992; Marcotte and Zhu, 1996; Marcotte, 1983) presented heuristics for

3

CNDP on the basis of system optimal approach and obtained good numerical results. However, these heuristics have not been extensively tested on large-scale networks generally.

## 2.1. Vulnerability indicators

The availability and quality of alternative routes is a very important indicator of vulnerability. The availability of spare capacity (capacity minus the flow) also could be an important indicator of vulnerability. Other examples could be v/c ratio, number of OD-pairs that use a link, number of vehicles affected by spillback (the spare capacity can be used to bypass an incident), extra vehicle kilometers travelled as a result of link closure, travel time losses as a result of crashes.

Snelder et al. (Snelder, n.d.) presented a topological vulnerability indicator. In her model, if (a) is the link where the disruption occurs, and (a)' is (a) link from the collection A of links that form an alternative for link (a), the vulnerability index is comprised from the ratio of capacity (a), over the summation of capacities of (a)', multiplied by a function of shortest path between a and (a)', and importance of the distance. The links that cross a line perpendicular to (a), are considered to be an alternative for link (a), if they meet the following requirements: The absolute angle between the original link and the alternative link must be smaller than 60 degrees.

Robust network design is focused on the reduction of the impact of disruptions in terms of reliability, vulnerability and potentially resilience if the analysis over time is to be considered. Disruptions can be in the trip rates of demand matrix, travel times, capacity, availability, traffic signals, and even change in direction of a link. A network is more robust, if it can withstand unexpected disruptions.

Dziubinski and Goyal (Dziubiński and Goyal, 2013) studied various games between a designer and an adversary. The designer tries to form a network consisting of n links, which are costly to construct, and also protect a set of them. The adversary, on the other hand, tries to damage the network to the maximum of its capabilities. Perfect and imperfect information in different scenarios is assumed to be available to the designer. The difference is considered as the knowledge of the designer of the possible moves of adversary, which depends on their payoffs. Their main finding was with limited available resources, the best defense would be in sparse networks, rather than centralized.

Murray-Tuite and Mahmassani (Murray-Tuite and Mahmassani, 2004) studied four types of games between a transportation operation manager of a network, and an adversary entity who tries to damage the network, using bi-level formulation. In their method, for each link a, the summation of vulnerability indices of all O/Ds with respect to link a, is considered as the vulnerability index of link a. This value is based on the utility of alternative routes, considering the current flow, and ratio of flow over demand. The utility in their paper is based on the ratio of free flow travel time over marginal travel time, and the relative capacity. Its value ranges from 0 to 1, where 1 indicates that the link is extremely important to the connectivity of that O/D.

Martin and Thesis (Martin and Thesis, 2007) studied various types of network design against attacks, and developed a tri-level defender attacker defender model to design a robust network, which in the inner model, the defender tries to minimize the users' costs. The proposed framework assumes that the defender at the outer level uses limited defensive resources to protect a system from attacks. At the middle level, the attacker uses their limited resources to attack the unprotected components while at the inner level the defender operates the system to minimize operating costs from damage (resulting from the attacker).

## 3. METHODOLOGY AND MODEL FORMULATION

As mentioned before, consideration of the vulnerabilities of networks against intelligent disruptions is crucial to alleviate the consequences of such events. The vulnerability can be evaluated by measuring the increase in the total system travel time[1]. This way, the damage due to the disturbance are viewed over the whole system.

To formulate the models, the sets, parameters, and variables are defined in Table 1. The notations are similar to model and graph representations in (Urban transportation networks, n.d.), and are adopted for the proposed models.

**Table 1: Notations**

Sets and Indices:

| | |
|---|---|
| $\mathcal{A}$ | Set of links |
| $\mathcal{N}$ | Set of Nodes |
| $\mathcal{R}$ | Set of origin nodes; $\forall \mathcal{R} \in \mathcal{N}$ |
| $\mathcal{S}$ | Set of destination nodes; $\forall \mathcal{S} \in \mathcal{N}$ |
| $\mathcal{K}_{rs}$ | The complete set of available paths connecting (O/D) pairs $r - s, \forall r \in \mathcal{R}, \forall s \in \mathcal{S}$ in the network |
| $q_{rs}$ | Demand between each Origin-Destination (O/D) pair $r - s, \forall r \in \mathcal{R}, \forall s \in \mathcal{S}$ |
| $\lambda_{rs}$ | shortest path for O/D pair $rs$ |
| $n_{rs}$ | Number of O/D pairs in the network |

Parameters:

| | |
|---|---|
| $\alpha_a$ | Constant, varying by facility type (BPR function) |
| $\beta_a$ | Constant, varying by facility type (BPR function) |
| $t_a^o$ | Free flow path travel time for link $a$ (hr) |
| $h_a$ | The capacity of each lane (veh/hr/ln) |
| MP | A multiplier constant number to give high cost for vehicles for using the target link |
| $B_d$ | Total budget/resources available to the designer |
| $B_z$ | Total budget/resources available to the adversary |
| $C_a$ | The capacity for link $a$ |
| $l_a$ | The number of lanes in link $a$ |
| $d_a$ | length for link $a$ |

Variables:

| | |
|---|---|
| $g_a(y_a)$ | improvement cost function for link $a$ |
| $t_a$ | Flow dependent link travel time on link $a$ (hr) |
| $f_k^{rs}$ | Flow on path $k$, connecting each origin-destination (O-D) pair $r - s, \forall r \in \mathcal{R}, \forall s \in \mathcal{S}$ |
| $\delta_{ak}^{rs}$ | $\delta_{a,k}^{rs} = 1$ if route $k$ between OD pair $r - s$ contains link $a$, and equal to 0 otherwise |
| $x_a$ | Total link flow (vph) on link $a$ |
| $y_a$ | Integer decision variable; total number of lanes to be added/expanded to link $a$ |
| $z_a$ | Binary decision variable; 1 if link $a$ is disabled, and 0 if it is not |

The model can be better understood using game theory concepts. Game theory provides mathematical tools for analyzing situations in which parties, called players, make independent

---
[1] Total System Travel Time

5

decisions. A game is defined as a finite game when each player has a finite number of options, the number of players is finite, and the game cannot go on indefinitely. It can be defined as the study of mathematical models of conflict and cooperation between intelligent rational decision makers. A solution to a game is the optimal decisions of the players, who may have similar, conflicting or mixed interest and the outcomes that may results from these decisions.

The problem and the solutions could be viewed from the aspect of three main players involved: the designer of the network, the users of it, and adversary entity. Frameworks can be defined based on one or more of these players. The usage of any of these frameworks differs by the involved players, order of moves and etc.

## 4. MODEL FORMULATION

Concentrating on reducing the effects of potential disruptions to the network, may distract the investments from definite reduction of the total system cost under normal conditions, and to invest on infrastructures that might never be beneficial (if no disruptions occur in future). Hence, an intellectual approach would be considering both aspects of reducing the system wide cost, and the potential vulnerabilities simultaneously. The aim of the designer/defender is to invest on projects such that the social welfare and robustness of the network are maximized simultaneously. The methodology presents a bi-objective formulation for the road network planner to model the cooperation of the goals.

The first move is completed by the designer of the network who has the advantage of putting his decision in place, and observing the reaction of the other players. The designer decision is defined by vector $y$. The value of $y_a$ shows the amount of expanding the capacity of link a. In this research, $y_a$ is the number of lanes to be added to link a. In the proposed model, it is assumed that the adversary entity finds the maximum possible damage to the network. His decision in the model is defined as vector z. The value of $z_a = 1$ shows the state to which link $a$ is damged and not available to the users; otherwise, the link is not affected. The damage is evaluated as the increase in the total system travel time. After the decisions of the designer and the adversary were made, the users of the network complete the next move. The reaction of the users is modeled using user equilibrium principles. The bi-level formulation models the relationship between the network manipulated by designer and adversary at the upper level, and the users at the lower level problem.

At designer level, the objective is to minimize the vulnerability of the network, by investing the available budget/resources in the expansion of the current capacity of links, by adding new lanes. Therefore, the designer makes his decision by adding new lanes to the network, considering his budget as a constraint. Then, the model examines the maximum damage that an adversary can inflict on the network, by incapacitating the links. Again, the model considers the limitation on adversary's available resources/budget. The value of the payoff can be considered as the TSTT. Therefore, the adversary can look for the damage which results in the maximum possible travel time of users of the system.

The general formulation for this model is presented in equations (1) through (5).

$$\min_{y} D(x(y), y)$$

$$1)$$

$$\min_{y} D'(x'(y, z(y)), y, z(y))$$

$$\text{s.t. } max_z \, A(x'(z), y, z) \tag{2}$$

$$min_x \, U(x, y) \tag{3}$$

$$\text{s.t.} \quad min_{x'} \, U'(x', y, z) \tag{4}$$

$$\tag{5}$$

In which $z(y)$ is the solution to the problem $A$ in equations (3) and (5); likewise $x(y)$ and $x'(y, z)$ are the solutions to the problems $U$ and $U'$ in equations (4) and (5) respectively. Statements (1) and (2) form a bi-objective problem, which tries to reduce the total system cost of the network at normal condition (before attack) and at degraded condition (after attack). The model formulation is written in equations (6) through (24).

$$\min_{y \in \mathbb{R}^n} \sum_{a \in A} x_a t_a(x_a, y_a), \qquad \forall a \in A \tag{6}$$

L1

$$\min_{y \in \mathbb{R}^n} \sum_{a \in A} \acute{x}_a \acute{t}_a(\acute{x}_a, y_a, z_a), \qquad \forall a \in A \tag{7}$$

$$\text{s.t.} \quad \sum_{a \in A} g_a(y_a) \leq B_d \tag{8}$$

$$g_a(y_a) = y_a . d_a \ , \quad \forall a \in A \tag{9}$$

$$y_a \geq 0, \ \forall a \in A \tag{10}$$

$$x_a = argmin_{x_a} \sum_{a \in A} \int_0^{x_a} t_a(w_a, y_a, z_a) dw \tag{11}$$

$$\text{s.t.} \quad t_a(x_a, y_a) = t_a^o \left[ 1 + \beta_a \left( \frac{x_a}{(y_a + C_a).h_a} \right)^\alpha \right] \tag{12}$$

$$\sum_{k \in \mathcal{K}} f_k^{rs} = q_{rs} \quad \forall r, s \tag{13}$$

$$x_a = \sum_{r-s} \sum_{k \in \mathcal{K}} \delta_{a,k}^{rs} f_k^{rs} \quad \forall a \in A \tag{14}$$

$$f_k^{rs} \geq 0 \ \forall k, r, s \tag{15}$$

$$q_{rs} \geq 0 \ \forall r, s \tag{16}$$

$$z_a = argmax_{z_a} \sum_{z \in \mathbb{Z}^n} \acute{x}_a \acute{t}_a(\acute{x}_a, y_a, z_a) , \ \forall a \in A \tag{17}$$

$$\text{s.t.} \quad \acute{x}_a = argmin_{\acute{x}_a} \sum_{a \in A} \int_0^{x_a} \acute{t}_a(w_a, y_a, z_a) dw \tag{18}$$

L3

$$\acute{t}_a(\acute{x}_a, y_a, z_a) = t_a^o \left[ 1 + \beta_a \left( \frac{\acute{x}_a}{(y_a + l_a).h_a} \right)^\alpha \right] . (1 + M_a . z_a) \tag{19}$$

$$\sum_{k \in \mathcal{K}} \acute{f}_k^{rs} = \acute{q}_{rs} \quad \forall r, s \tag{20}$$

$$\acute{x}_a = \sum_{r-s} \sum_{k \in \mathcal{K}} \delta_{a,k}^{rs} \acute{f}_k^{rs} \quad \forall a \in A \tag{21}$$

$$\acute{f}_k^{rs} \geq 0 \ \forall k, r, s \tag{22}$$

$$\acute{q}_{rs} \geq 0 \ \forall r, s \tag{23}$$

$$\sum_{a \in A} z_a \leq B_z \tag{24}$$

$$\acute{t}_a(\acute{x}_a, y_a, z_a) = t_a^0 \left[ 1 + \beta_a \left( \frac{\acute{x}_a}{(y_a + l_a).h_a} \right)^\alpha \right] . (1 + M_a . z_a) \tag{25}$$

$$\sum_{k \in \mathcal{K}} \acute{f}_k^{rs} = \acute{q}_{rs} \quad \forall r, s \tag{26}$$

$$\acute{x}_a = \sum_{r-s} \sum_{k \in \mathcal{K}} \acute{\delta}_{a,k}^{rs} \acute{f}_k^{rs} \quad \forall a \in A \tag{27}$$

The defender/designer of the network not only minimizes the overall cost to users, similar to the conventional urban network design problems, but also they attempt to reduce the potential effect of any intelligent adversary movements. The decision of the designer, implicitly affects the behavior of the users, and the potential moves of the adversary entity. Therefore, the hierarchy of decision flow, starts from the designer at level $L1$. There are two players in the next sequence of the hierarchy structure of decision makers, $L2$, a user player for the normal condition of the network, and an adversary. The network modified by the adversary, provides data for the last player in the hierarchy sequence of decisions, $L3$. Hence, the network defender has two objectives, the minimization of a performance measure like total system travel cost, and also at the same time the minimization of vulnerabilities. This behavior was represented in the user level which is based on Wardrop's first principle, saying that no user can experience a lower travel time by unilaterally changing his/her routes. Thus, the road users desire to separately select their routes such that their individual travel costs are minimized while the planners look for the best link improvements within the network but have no control over the users' route choices. Similar rules apply to adversary-user interactions.

In equations (6) through (24), two separate user equilibrium problems are defined. The first one is in the second level of optimization, which provides information regarding the flow in an undamaged network. The second one is at the third level, which feeds the adversary problem with information about the degraded network. The variables for the second user equilibrium problem is differentiated using the apostrophe after the variables' letters. The nonlinear programming model for the first user equilibrium problem is provided in equations (11) through (16). Equation (11) denotes the objective function of the UE problem. Constraint (13) describes the demand conservation condition. That is to say, all trips should be assigned to the network. The flow on all routes between each OD pair, has to be equal to the OD trip rate. Constraint (14) outlines the relation between flows on links and route(s), for each OD. The binary value of $\delta_{a,k}^{rs}$ is 1, when link $a$ is on the path $k$, and it is zero otherwise. Constraint (15) and (16) satisfies the non-negativity of path flow and travel demand correspondingly, so the solutions are physically meaningful. Similarly, the second user equilibrium are presented in equations (18) through (23). Constraint (8) represents the total available budget $B_d$ for network capacity improvements. Similarly, Constraint (24) shows the limitation on the number of elements that adversary entity can damage.

## 5. SOLUTION ALGORITHM

Three optimization tasks should be addressed for the three players in the model. The designer of the network should search over the best possible solutions for the design of the network while the adversary should move after the designer and search to find the most crucial links of the network to be degraded or completely disabled. And the last move is done by the users of the network who individually search for the best route for themselves in terms of the least travel time.

The overall flowchart of the solution algorithms for the three decision makers is presented in Figure 1. It should be noted that to keep the diagram simple, the convergence criteria for user level problems is not demonstrated in this figure.

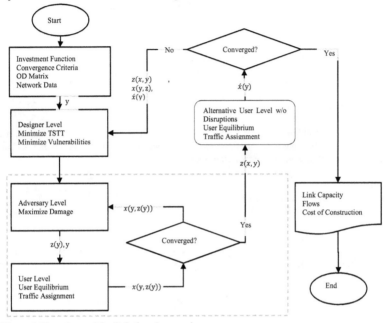

Figure 1 Flowchart of the Solution Approach

The algorithms that have been used for each level are discussed in the following sections.

## 5.1. Algorithm for Users

Since the user level problem is a nonlinear derivable convex problem, it can be solved using efficient heuristic algorithms like the Frank Wolfe algorithm (FW), algorithm B, gradient descent and other gradient based algorithms. The Frank Wolfe algorithm is also known as reduced gradient and convex combination algorithm. The model formulation is provided in equations (11) through (16).. The Frank Wolfe heuristic search algorithm is used for convergence of the objective function to its optimal value using the associated direction vector's move size. The objective function is the sum of the integrals of the link performance functions. The steps of the Frank Wolfe algorithm are as follows:

**Step 0**: Initialization
Perform all-or-nothing assignment based on $t_a = t_a(0) \; \forall a$. A new flow vector $\{x_a\}$ will be generated. Set counter $n = 1$.

**Step 1**: Update

Set $t_a = t_a(x_a) \; \forall a$

**Step 2:** Finding Direction
Perform all-or-nothing assignment based on $\{t_a\}$. A new auxiliary flow vector $\{x'_a\}$ will be generated.

**Step 3:** Line search
Find $\alpha_n$ ($0 \leq \alpha \leq 1$) that solves equation (28):

$$\min z(x) = \sum_a \int_0^{x_a + \alpha(x'^n_a - x^n_a)} t_a(w)dw \tag{28}$$

The line search problem is solved using bisection algorithm (Bolzano search). The converge criteria for the bisection method is defined as the distance between the lower bound and upper bound of the current section in bisection iterations.

**Step 4:** Move
Move to the new solution using equation (29).
$$x_a^{n+1} = x_a^n + \alpha_n (x'^n_a - x^n_a), \forall a \tag{29}$$

**Step 5:** Convergence test
If the convergence criterion is met, stop and accept the current solution $\{x_a^{n+1}\}$, as the set of equilibrium link flows. If the convergence criterion is not met, set $n = n + 1$ and go to step 1. The convergence is tested using equation (30):
$$\frac{\sqrt{\sum_a (x_a^{n+1} - x_a^n)^2}}{\sum_a x_a^n} \leq k \tag{30}$$

The Frank Wolfe algorithm is relatively simple to implement and has a fast convergence in the first iterations. Since the update step is "one-at-a-time" generically, it is not parallelizable for better computational performance.

## 5.2. Algorithm for Designer/Defender and Adversary

In this research, decisions of the designer and adversary are considered to be discrete. In addition, since their objectives are nonlinear and non-convex, they fall into the category of NP hard problems. Therefore, efficient exact and heuristic solutions do not exist, and approximate algorithms like meta-heuristic algorithms would be the best approach for medium and large scale sizes of these types of problems. Meta-heuristics are a subfield of stochastic optimization that combine basic heuristic methods in higher level frameworks, and their goal is to search effectively and efficiently. They are especially suited for problems with imperfect or incomplete information or limited computation capacity. One of the population based meta-heuristics is the category of evolutionary computations' (EC) algorithms; and one of the best known and efficient categories of EC's algorithms is the genetic algorithm (GA). A genetic algorithm is a search heuristic that mimics the procedure of natural selection. The GA works by evolving a population of candidate solutions, also known as individuals or phenotypes, toward better solutions. Each candidate solution has a set of properties which is its chromosome or also known as genotype. Its process routinely produces a new population by mutating and altering the current population. Each population, called a generation, contains the candidate solutions.

The problem size can vary based on the number of the links in the network, number of the lanes, number of nodes, and improvement approaches. A genetic algorithm is specially suited to deal with multi-objective problems. The chromosomal representation for the designer and adversary is described in the next section. The problem of the upper level can be defined as a multi-objective problem. In a multi-objective problem, more than one objective is optimized at the same time. A good solution approach would be combining the objectives of the designer and adversary into a monotonic objective function which has the set of variables of both which can be solved using a GA.

The designer's objective function result will be a trial additional number of lanes vector ($y_a$). The designer's decision variables are limited by the budget and resources constraints. The decisions of the designer and adversary modifies the network, and passes it to the next player in the defined sequence of decision flow. The pseudo code of the algorithm is presented briefly as follows:

**Step 0: Initialization.** Create initial random population of organisms (potential solution)

**Step 1: Evaluate.** Evaluate fitness of each organism/chromosome
For the adversary, the fitness value is based on running traffic assignment on the degraded network, defined by the individual adversary solutions.
For the designer, the fitness value is based on the new design of network defined by the individual designer solutions, which might be degraded by the adversary as a median player.

**Step 2: Convergence criterion.** If the fitness for all evaluated organisms is considered as a good solution, then the procedure is finished. Otherwise go to step 3.

**Step 3: Exploit.** Eliminate the weak organisms and produce new organisms based on individuals in the population with better fitness.

**Step 4: Explore.** Stochastically mutate organisms' genes. Then repeat the process starting at step 1.

### 5.3. Decoding and Chromosomal Representation

Decoding is about representing the genotypes in a real phenotype feasible space. Each individual variable when encoded into genotype, is converted to the real representation value of the objective function. So the output of the decoding function, makes the suitable variables for inserting to the objective function(s). A computationally efficient representation for chromosomes, is a one dimensional series of binary variables. A simple example of decoding a binary representation of the chromosomes for the designer and adversary, using 3 bits of data, for 3 links is presented in Figure 2.

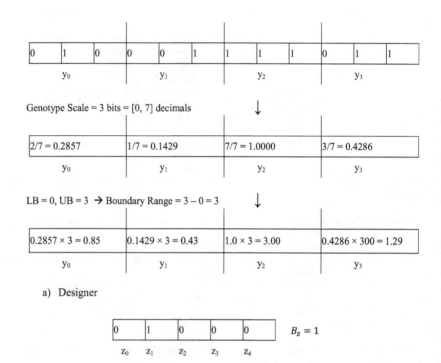

a) Designer

b) adversary entity

Figure 2 Decoding procedure and genotype chromosome representation

In the defined encoding/decoding procedure, the actual genome in a genetic algorithm process is first converted into a real representation value ranging from 0 to 1.0. This representation value can be used as a general form that can be scaled to any desired boundary defined by the specific problem. Depending on the boundaries defined by the specific problem, the real representation value can scale the output of a genetic algorithm to the size of decision variables of the problem. The decision maker should be aware of the boundaries of the decision variables of their problem. So they can be confident that the genetic algorithm progress would not miss any solutions because of not being able to touch all the feasible space of the problem. In the above example, each variable is encoded into 3 bits of data. So, the scale of genotype of each variable is ranging from 0 to 1. The boundaries of the phenotype variables in the actual problem are defined by the feasible space of the problem. In this case, each non-negative variable has a maximum value of 3 as their upper-level value. This value in the next step, is used to scale the genotype value range to the actual feasible space range. If the required decoded variable is discrete, the decoded value can be rounded to the closest integer value. The constraint of the adversary entity, which is the number of links that can be affected by its problem, can implemented in the decoding/encoding procedure.

In this approach, the alleles with binary value one in the corresponding chromosomes, represent the attacked links. The upper bound of the adversary budget constraint, is defined by the summation or equivalently the total number of 1s in the corresponding chromosomes. To have the problem feasible, in the solution algorithms the mutation operators should be avoided. The moves in the genotype space can be performed by cross-over operators.

To test the algorithm, and perform sensitivity analysis on the properties of the genetic algorithm, bi-level network design problems were defined for two small test networks. The network configurations is described in the next sections. The objective functions in network design problems are usually minimization. Therefore a ranked based roulette is a good approach for the selection. The population size for the both problems is 100 individuals.

## 6. NUMERICAL EXPERIMENTS

Numerical experiments were conducted in order to evaluate the performance of the method and observe the results. The designer and adversary level algorithm were coded and solved using MATLAB, and the user level algorithm was implemented in C++. The method was processed on a computer with an Intel i7-960 processor and 24GB of RAM.

Numerical experiments are conducted for the Sioux Falls in order to evaluate the proposed methodology. The network consists of 76 links, and 24 nodes which are also defined as the demand origin/destinations. It is assumed that all the links in the initial network have three lanes. The links attributes and OD trips were adopted from (Suwansirikul et al., 1987). Similar to test network 1, two scenarios were performed on this network using different budgets available to the adversary.

Figure 3 demonstrates the 14 candidate links that are selected for improvements (Link numbers 13, 23, 30, 51, 27, 32, 34, 40, 49, 52, 53, 58, 39 and 74).

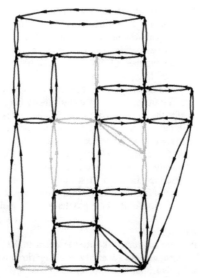

Figure 3 Links Included in Expansion (links with green color) for the Sioux Falls network

### 6.1. Adversary budget = 1

For the first experiment, the attacker upper bound was limited to 1 link. The three level algorithm was used to solve this problem. The designer level problem is a bi-objective problem of minimizing the total system travel time, and the total system travel time of the damaged network, which is obtained by solving the attacker problem in the second level of the model.

The designer decision is limited by the construction budget which is available to them. In this experiment, the budget is assumed to be 20 million dollars. Their decision of adding lanes to the current links is also constrained by an upper bound of a maximum of 3 lanes per link.

For the designer and attacker problem, a population size of 100 individuals/chromosomes is considered. For both problems, in the optimization process, 100 of generations were populated by the individuals in each iteration. In this example, the optimal solution found was adding one lane to link 23, 34, 39, 40, 49, 53, 58, and adding two lanes to links 13, 27, 32, 51, 52, 74 and adding three lanes to link 30.

The final decision of the designer is represented in Figure 5. The optimal decision of the adversary entity under the initial network is attacking link 43, while its target changes to link 25 in the improved network conditions. The numbers on links shows the total number of lanes to be added to the links. The initial total system travel time under normal conditions is reduced from $7.48 \times 10^6$ minute to $5.98 \times 10^6$ minutes in the improved network. Considering the degraded network after the attack, the total system travel time is $7.80 \times 10^6$. This value is comparable to the value for the initial network after attack which is $10.89 \times 10^6$. Figure 4 presents the changes in the total system travel time after the improvement. The additional system cost due to the attacks are represented by red stacks over the network under normal condition, which represented by blue bars. The addition of the new lanes to the network, could reduce the total system travel time by 20.1 percent. However, the improvement by the proposed model is more significant by looking at vulnerability aspects. The new improved network could reduce the imposed additional system cost from $3.41 \times 10^6$ minutes to $1.82 \times 10^6$, which is 46.4 percent.

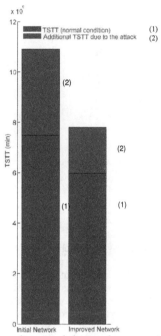

Figure 4 Improvement of the capacity expanded network compare to the initial conditions

## 6.2. Adversary budget = 2

The second experiment considers that two links can be damaged by the adversary entity. The individual solutions by generations are provided in Figure 5. Similar to the previous case, the chromosomes move toward the best solutions during the process of evolutionary optimization.

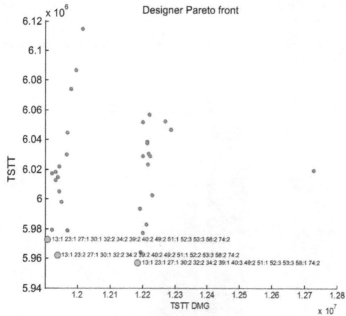

Figure 5 Individuals solutions at by the two objectives of the designer at the 100[st] generation

Figure 5 presents the individual solutions at the 100th generations. The red dots, represent the Pareto frontier solutions. The solutions with bad fitness values are removed during the process of the genetic algorithm. In the last iteration, all the individuals are confined to the best solutions. The best decision for the designer is to choose a solution from the Pareto front of the last generation.

Figure 6 presents the optimal solution of the adversary entity correspond to the best defender decision. The optimal solution found for the adversary was changed from link 43 and 60 in the initial network, to 23 and 27 in the improved network.

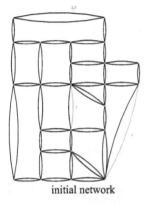 

initial network                              improved network

**Figure 6 the optimal decisions of the attacker for the initial and improved networks**

Compared to the results of the previous experiment, links 34, 40, 52, 53 and 58 are collecting more investment in this test. The total system travel time for the initial network, and the improved network are $7.48\times10^6$ minutes and $5.97\times10^6$ minutes respectively. The values for the degraded network are $13.53\times10^6$ minutes before improvements, and $11.90\times10^6$ minutes after the improvements. Giving a higher budget to the adversary entity, in terms of damaging the network elements, creates a larger total cost to the users.

Since the damage to the links is modeled by increasing the travel time to a higher value, the travelers are not interested in using these links. However, there still exist low traffic volumes that use these links in the degraded network. This is due to the fact that the degree of damage to the network, in this test, is significant enough that a portion of users utilize these links despite the higher cost. In other words, the damages to the mentioned links, create high congestion on some of the alternative routes. The improved network, influences drivers to use links other than centralized links. Hence, the potential damages that the attacker can incur on the whole network would be minimized.

## 7. CONCLUSION

A quantitative method for ranking their projects for budget allocation is essential for transportation agencies. The objective of allocation of these resources can generally be the maximization of social welfare. An intelligent adversary may look for vulnerabilities in the network to degrade its performance. At the planner's level, allocating resources without considering the potential of disruptions by the intelligent adversary, may not help reduce the vulnerabilities, or similarly increase the robustness of the network. To address this issue, models were presented for designing robust networks. The models were formed in multi-level optimization, considering flows of decisions are to be made in sequence. Therefore, a hierarchy structure of the movements are presented. The planner of the network is assumed to look for investing the assigned budget on the links/projects of the network, while the enemy was assumed to damages/disable links. The results of the optimization of these players are passed to the lower level. The lower level problem provides flow vectors based on user equilibrium principles. The interaction between these levels forms multi-level problems. A solution algorithm is presented based on genetic algorithms for the network designer and attacker, and Frank Wolfe for the users. Several test networks were examined to evaluate the performance of the algorithms and models. The results showed that the proposed model can search over the possible results for the designer and choose the most robust solution compare to the other possible solutions. Results showed promising achievements in terms of increasing the robustness of the network against intelligent disruptions, and also improving other system wide performance measures as presented in the bi-objective robust network design problem model.

## 8. REFERENCES

Allsop, R.E., 1974. Some possibilities for using traffic control to influence trip distribution and route choice, in: Transportation and Traffic Theory, Proceedings.

Chiou, S.-W., 2005a. Bilevel programming for the continuous transport network design problem. Transp. Res. Part B Methodol. 39, 361–383. doi:10.1016/j.trb.2004.05.001

Chiou, S.-W., 2005b. Bilevel programming for the continuous transport network design problem. Transp. Res. Part B Methodol. 39, 361–383. doi:10.1016/j.trb.2004.05.001

Dziubiński, M., Goyal, S., 2013. Network design and defence. Games Econ. Behav. 79, 30–43. doi:10.1016/j.geb.2012.12.007

Gershwin, S.B., Tan, H.-N., others, 1979. Hybrid Optimization: control of traffic networks in equilibrium.

Konur, D., Golias, M.M., Darks, B., 2013. A mathematical modeling approach to resource allocation for railroad-highway crossing safety upgrades. Accid. Anal. Prev. 51, 192–201. doi:10.1016/j.aap.2012.11.011

Leblanc, L.J., 1973. Mathematical programming algorithms for large scale network equilibrium and network design problems.

Marcotte, P., 1983. Network Optimization with Continuous Control 17, 181–197.

Marcotte, P., 1986. Network design problem with congestion effects: A case of bilevel programming. Math. Program. 34, 142–162.

Marcotte, P., Marquis, G., 1992. Efficient implementation of heuristics for the continuous network design problem. Ann. Oper. Res. 34, 163–176.

Marcotte, P., Zhu, D.L., 1996. Exact and inexact penalty methods for the generalized bilevel programming problem. Math. Program. 74, 141–157. doi:10.1007/BF02592209

Martin, P.A.S., Thesis, 2007. TRI-LEVEL OPTIMIZATION MODELS TO DEFEND CRITICAL INFRASTRUCTURE.

Murray, A.T., Davis, R., Stimson, R.J., Ferreira, L., 1998. Public Transportation Access. Transp. Res. Part D Transp. Environ. 3, 319–328. doi:10.1016/S1361-9209(98)00010-8

Murray-Tuite, P., Mahmassani, H., 2004. Methodology for Determining Vulnerable Links in a Transportation Network. Transp. Res. Rec. 1882, 88–96. doi:10.3141/1882-11

Snelder, M., n.d. Designing Robust Road Networks.

Steenbrink, P.A., 1974. Optimization of transport networks. New York.

Suwansirikul, C., Friesz, T.L., Tobin, R.L., 1987. Equilibrium Decomposed Optimization: A Heuristic for the Continuous Equilibrium Network Design Problem. Transp. Sci. 21, 254–263. doi:10.1287/trsc.21.4.254